The Bruge

and

Beer Guide

All rights reserved. No part of this publication may be reproduced, stored in a retrieval system or transmitted in any form without the prior written permission of the author.

With grateful thanks to Chris Pinnock and Lee Barnes.

Every effort has been made to ensure the contents of this book are correct at the time of publication. Nevertheless, the publisher cannot be held responsible for any errors or omissions, or for the consequences of any reliance on the information provided by the same. This does not affect your statutory rights.

(c) 2017 Robert Frosdick

If you would like to suggest a bar for inclusion or provide updated information regarding an entry, please email feedback@nssales.co.uk

Welcome to Bruges

Bruges (Brugge) is an extremely picturesque Belgium city. It has such a well preserved historic centre that it can feel like you are walking through an outdoor museum. It is easily reached by the train to Bruges station followed by a short walk to the city centre. By car Bruges is on the N9 and N50 roads and a short distance from the E40 and E403 motorways.

With its abundance of canals Bruges is often dubbed the 'Venice of the North' and combined with the large number of medieval buildings, the entire centre of the city has been deservedly awarded UNESCO World Heritage Site status. The compact city centre contains the beautiful medieval squares the Grote Markt and the Burg, which are surrounded by impressive merchant houses, churches, a stunning Bell Tower and the Town Hall.

In this handy guide, we've provided details of what we consider to be the Top 10 best beer bars/cafes to visit during your stay. You'll also find details of the breweries that are open for tours, the top monuments, attractions and museums that you can visit and the best bottle shops in town. Our aim is to provide the perfect companion for any keen beer tourist during their stay.

Bruges Bars

1. 't Brugs Beertje, Kemelstraat 5. Open Monday, Thursday and Friday 4pm to Midnight. Saturday and Sunday 4pm to 1am. Closed Tuesday and Wednesday. Some bar snacks available. www.brugsbeertje.be

This renowned beer bar, known as "Bruges's Little Bear", has built an enviable reputation for serving top quality Belgium beer since it opened in 1983. The beer menu contains around 300 different types and you are sure to find yourself surrounded by a like-minded crowd of appreciative beer lovers. **TOP CHOICE**

2. Cambrinus, Philipstockstraat 19. Open all week 11am to 11pm - although often open later. Food available. www.cambrinus.eu

Cambrinus was a legendary king credited with the invention of beer, who is often given the title the "King of Beer". With around 400 bottles on their menu this stylish beer brasserie does him proud. Housed in an impressive building dating from 1699 and with a decent food menu as well, we highly recommend you give it a visit. **TOP CHOICE**

3. De Garre, De Garre 1. Open daily 12noon to Midnight. 12noon to 1am on Friday and Saturday. Some bar snacks available. www.degarre.be

Tucked away in a side alley near the Belfry it's easy to overlook this quaint little bar. Their beer list contains around 130 choices including the rather nice house beer De Garre Tripel which is brewed exclusively for them by the Van Steenberge brewery.

4. 't Poatersgat, Vlamingstraat 82. Open daily 5pm to 1am, sometimes later. Some bar snacks available.

This lively bar is somewhat of a hidden gem being based in the cellar of a nineteenth century church. If you manage to find the bar the search will be worthwhile as the beer list contains an excellent range over 100 choices.

5. Le Trappiste, Kuipersstraat 33. Closed Monday. Open 5pm to Midnight all other days. Some bar snacks available. www.belgianbeer.wixsite.com/letrappiste

Opening in 2013, this relatively new entry into the Bruges bar scene has rapidly gained an enviable reputation. There are more than 100 beers on the menu, including an interesting range of international craft and micro-brewed beers. Set in an atmospheric 13th Century cellar with friendly and knowledgeable staff on hand to help if required, this is a highly recommended bar to try. **TOP CHOICE**

6. Café Rose Red, Cordoeaniersstraat 16. Closed Monday. Open all other days 11am to Midnight. Food available. www.cordoeanier.be/rosered.php

This attractive cafe features red roses hanging from the beams to live up to its name. It is attached to the Hotel Cordoeanier but it is open to anyone and has a lovely terrace for when the weather is nice. They offer around 150 beers, including a *beer of the month*, but their speciality is beers from trappist breweries. There are now only seven brewers left who can carry the logo 'Authentic Trappist Product' on their bottles and six of those are based in Belgium. The label not only certifies the monastic origins of the product but also guarantees that the products sold comply with the required quality and tradition. As a result you can expect to find a good range of beers from the likes of Achel, Westmalle, Chimay and Rochefort always available.

7. Duvelorium Grand Beer Café, Markt 1. Open daily from 10am to 6pm and Thursdays from 10am to 9pm. www.historium.be

The Duvelorium is the only bar in the world dedicated to the famous Belgian Duvel beer. The bar is located upstairs in the Historium, an interactive museum in which visitors are taken on a fascinating journey into the thriving city of Bruges in the year 1435. You don't need to visit the museum to try the Duvelorium, just head upstairs to find this impressive bar. Beers offered normally include Duvel, Vedett, Achouffe, Liefmans and De Koninck, and you'll often find special limited edition Duvel brews. Make sure to check out the fantastic views of the Grote Markt from the balcony. There is also a beer gift shop if you fancy taking a bottle or two away.

8. @The Pub, Hallestraat 4. Closed Tuesday. Open Friday, Saturday and Sunday 4pm to late. All other days 5pm to 1am. Food available.

If you overlook the rather touristy sign declaring "@ The Pub - The Place To Be" you will be rewarded with a decent bar that has over 100 beers on the menu. There are plenty of seats out the front when the weather is good.

9. 2Be + The Beerwall, Wollestraat 53. Open all week 9.30am to 7.30pm. Snack food served. www.2-be.biz

The entrance to the 2Be Bar and Bottle shop is the amazing Beer Wall; a massive display of different Belgium beer bottles and glasses, which is well worth a visit on its own. The bar itself offers around 50 beers including 16 rotating draft beers. The attached bottle shop stocks an impressive 400 different beers along with various other Belgium novelties. **TOP CHOICE**

10. Yesterday's World, Wijngaardstraat 6. Open daily from 2pm to midnight. Snack food served. This unusual bar scores highly on the novelty value. Combining a pub with an antiques shop is rather a fun idea, so if you like the look of any of the knick-knacks and ornaments that surround the room you can buy them along with your beer. Yesterday's World is a quirky bar that is well worth a visit and with around 65 beers you won't go thirsty while your browse.

Bruges Restaurant Choice

In addition to the bars that serve food on the previous pages, there are a couple of other restaurants we have come across that we feel are worthy of a special mention.

11. Ribs 'n Beer, Ezelstraat 50. Open daily 6pm to late. www.ribsnbeer.com
There is a lot more on the menu than just ribs, but the 'all you can eat ribs' with chocolate and beer sauce is hard to refuse. The beer list is fairly good as well.

12. Jilles Beer & Burgers, Braambergstraat 10. Open daily 12noon to 9pm, although times can vary. See website for details www.jilles.be
Jilles is a small chain of gourmet burger restaurants with other branches in Ghent and Ostend. The burgers are delicious but as we are interested in beer, the bottle menu with over 45 choices, is unexpectedly good for a burger joint. The beers include some from the local Fort Lapin brewery (see below).
TOP CHOICE

The following breweries also have restaurants attached:
Bourgogne des Flandres, Kartuizerinnenstraat 6. (see below)
De Halve Maan Brewery, Walplein 26. (see below)

Bruges Breweries

13. De Halve Maan Brewery, Walplein 26. Tours are organised daily between 11am and 4pm and until 5pm on Saturdays. www.halvemaan.be

In 1564 the brewery 'Die Maene' was mentioned in the town register of Bruges. The Maes family took this over in 1856 to form the basis for the brewery that we know today. There have been several moves and changes of ownership since then, but the launch of the award winning Brugse Zot beer in 2005 has put the current brewers on a steady footing. In fact, production has expanded so much in recent years that the brewery crowd-funded the money to install a two-mile beer pipeline from the brewery to its bottling plant to avoid having so many lorries driving through the historic city centre. The brewery has a restaurant attached serving snacks and traditional Belgium cuisine between 12noon and 3pm. **TOP CHOICE**

14. Bourgogne des Flandres, Kartuizerinnenstraat 6. Closed Monday. All other days open 10am to 6pm. Tours can be booked at the entrance or in advance via the website; www.bourgognedesflandres.be

Bourgogne des Flandres is a typical example of the Flemish beer blending tradition with old and young beer being mixed judiciously to achieve a perfect balance. Bourgogne des Flandres Pure is brewed on site in the loft and blended with a lambic from the Timmermans Brewery. This lambic has aged for over twelve months in wooden barrels and the resulting blend is a delicious red-brown beer with a complex flavour. The beer was originally brewed in Bruges by the Den Os Brewery from 1825 until it closed in 1957. This new brewery which opened in 2015, is based just 50 metres from the location of the old brewery and re-establishes this distinct beer style back to where it belongs in the heart of Bruges. The brewery also features an impressive restaurant serving traditional Belgium cuisine to perfectly accompany their beer.

15. Fort Lapin Brewery, Koolkerkse Steenweg 32. Group tours can be arranged, contact the brewery for details. www.fortlapin.com
Just outside Bruges' city centre you'll find Fort Lapin, a small artisan brewery that produces a number of craft beers including tripel Fort Lapin 8 and quadrupel Fort Lapin 10. If you're not able to arrange a tour be sure to look out for their beers in the local bars or bottle shops.

Beer Festival

If you happen to be visiting in February be sure to check if the Bruges Beer Festival is being held (www.brugsbierfestival.be) during your trip. This impressive annual festival normally offers over 300 beers with beer tokens buying you 15cl samples.

Beer Bottle Shop

16. K&S Shops, 52 Katelijnestraat. Open daily from 10am to 7pm. www.kstobacco.be
This labyrinth of a shop sells a large range of tobacco, Bruges souvenirs and over 800 different types of beer. There is even a bar if you fancy a break from all the shopping.

17. The Bottle Shop, Wollestraat 13. Open daily from 10am to 6.30pm. www.thebottleshop.be
The Bottle Shop has been a landmark for beer lovers in Bruges for over 15 years. Conveniently located in the centre of town the shop stocks around 600 different beers along with Belgium spirits and other gift ideas.

18. De Biertempel, Philipstockstraat 7. Open daily from 10am to 7pm. www.biertempel.eu
Linked with the 'Beer Temple' shop in Brussels (Grasmarkt 56), this shrine to Belgium beer stocks around 600 different types.

See also: 9. 2Be + The Beerwall, Wollestraat 53 (above)

Top Attractions

A. Onze-Lieve-Vrouwekerk (Church of Our Lady), Mariastraat. Open daily 9.30 to 5pm. Sunday 1.30pm to 5pm. www.visitbruges.be

It's impossible to miss this stunning church. Its brick tower is over 120 meters tall and therefore quite literally the high point of Brugean building craft. Inside is no less impressive as the church holds an immense collection of religious art, artefacts and historic tombs. The most notable of these being the world-famous 'Madonna and Child' sculpture by Michelangelo. **TOP CHOICE**

B. Belfort, Markt 7. Open daily 9.30am to 6pm. www.visitbruges.be

Dating from the 13th century, Bruges's impressive bell-tower stands 83 meters above the city. Inside the tower 366 steps lead you to the top where a fabulous 47 bell carillon and fantastic views await. **TOP CHOICE**

C. Stadhuis, Burg 12. Open daily 9.30am to 5pm. www.visitbruges.be

On the south side of the Burg (one of Europe's finest medieval squares) you'll find the 14th century Stadhuis (Town Hall). This Gothic masterpiece is one of the oldest town halls in Belgium and inside contains the magnificent Gotische Zaal (Gothic Hall), which is well worth the price of admission.

D. Groeningemuseum, Dijver 12. Closed Mondays. Open all other days 9.30am to 5pm. www.visitbruges.be

The Groeninge Museum provides a varied overview of the history of Belgian visual art, with its renowned collections of the Flemish Primitives, Renaissance & Baroque masters, and 19th century realists. Highlights include The Virgin and Child with Canon Van der Paele by Jan van Eyck, Last Judgement by Hieronymus Bosch and the glorious Moreel Triptych by Hans Memling.

E. Choco-Story (Chocolate Museum), Wijnzakstraat 2. Open daily 10am to 5pm. www.choco-story-brugge.be

Why is Belgium so good at making delicious chocolates? This museum traces the history of cocoa and chocolate, right through from the Mayans and the Spanish conquistadores to the chocolate connoisseurs of today.

F. Bruges Beer Museum, Breidelstraat 3. Open daily 10am to 5pm. www.brugesbeermuseum.com

This hands-on and interactive museum tells you the story of beer in a fun and innovative way. You will learn about the history of beer from its beginnings until the present day, including beer in Bruges, Trappist beers, beer types and the brewing process. Best of all there is a tasting room at the end of the tour with great views over the market square. **TOP CHOICE**

***Historium, Markt 1.** This historical experience attraction, takes you back in time to medieval Bruges of the 15th century. See above; 7. Duvelorium Grand Beer Café.*

Take a Boat Trip. www.visitbruges.be
A visit to Bruges isn't complete without a boat trip on its pretty canals. Go aboard at any of the five landing stages that are easy to spot around the city centre for a half-hour trip where you will see the most interesting sights of the city. **TOP CHOICE**

Bruges City Map

1. 't Brugs Beertje, Kemelstraat 5.
2. Cambrinus, Philipstockstraat 19.
3. De Garre, De Garre 1.
4. 't Poatersgat, Vlamingstraat 82.
5. Le Trappiste, Kuipersstraat 33.
6. Café Rose Red, Cordoeaniersstraat 16.

7. Duvelorium Grand Beer Café, Markt 1.
8. @The Pub, Hallestraat 4.
9. 2Be + The Beerwall, Wollestraat 53.
10. Yesterday's World, Wijngaardstraat 6.
11. Ribs 'n Beer, Ezelstraat 50.
12. Jilles Beer & Burgers, Braambergstraat 10.
13. De Halve Maan Brewery, Walplein 26.
14. Bourgogne des Flandres, Kartuizerinnenstraat 6.
15. Fort Lapin Brewery, Koolkerkse Steenweg 32.
16. K&S Shops, 52 Katelijnestraat.
17. The Bottle Shop, Wollestraat 13.
18. De Biertempel, Philipstockstraat 7.

A. Onze-Lieve-Vrouwekerk (Church of Our Lady), Mariastraat.
B. Belfort, Markt 7.
C. Stadhuis, Burg 12.
D. Groeningemuseum, Dijver 12.
E. Choco-Story (Chocolate Museum), Wijnzakstraat 2.
F. Bruges Beer Museum, Breidelstraat 3.

NOTES

Printed in Great Britain
by Amazon